COUNTRY
LABORS

1.95   Nvs. 97

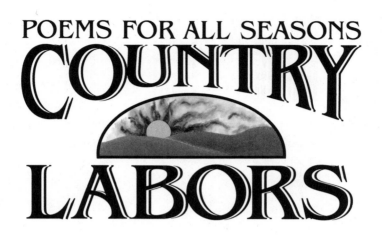

POEMS FOR ALL SEASONS
COUNTRY
LABORS

JOHN LEAX

ZondervanPublishingHouse
Grand Rapids, Michigan

A Division of HarperCollins*Publishers*

COUNTRY LABORS
Copyright © 1991 by John Leax

Requests for information should be addressed to:
Zondervan Publishing House
1415 Lake Drive S.E.
Grand Rapids, Michigan 49506

Library of Congress Cataloging-in-Publication Data

Leax, John.

    Country labors : new poems / by John Leax.
      p. cm.
    ISBN 0-310-53281-7
    1. Country life—Poetry. I. Title.
    PS3562.E262C68 1991   90-22022
    811'.54–dc20   CIP

Poems in this collection have appeared in the following periodicals: *Old Hickory Review, Christianity and Literature, Cream City Review, Anglican Theological Review, Sunrust, Kentucky Poetry Review,* and *Nimrod.*

"Thirst" originally appeared in *Tending the Garden: Essays on the Gospel and the Earth* edited by Wesley Granberg-Michaelson (Grand Rapids: Eerdmans, 1987).

Printed in the United States of America

91 92 93 / ML / 4 3 2 1

For Linda

Hands worn hard by labor give
better tongue to truth than words.

Come, work beside me.
Turn the garden earth to light.
Let hope be found in fact.

A Note on Parts One and Two

When I was a boy, I addressed both of my
grandfathers as "Pap." In writing these poems
I have continued that practice, for that is how
I think of them. In the poems of "Leax Lane,"
Pap always refers to my paternal grandfather.
In "Burning," Pap always refers to my
maternal grandfather.

Contents

I am convinced, that for the human soul to prosper in rustic life a certain vantage-ground is pre-requisite. It is not every man that is likely to be improved by a country life or by country labors. Education, or original sensibility, or both, must preexist, if the changes, forms, and incidents of nature are to prove a sufficient stimulant.

Samuel Taylor Coleridge, Biographia Literaria

I

LEAX LANE

Home is where one starts from . . .

T. S. Eliot, "East Coker"

Peeps: 1948

Inside the dark of early spring,
I trailed across the lane
and clambered up the ramp
behind Pap. As the door
swung open, yellow light
spilled, like cracked corn,
onto the yard. I stepped
through its welcome sweep
and followed Pap
into the chicken house it warmed.

Broody hens shifted and clucked
in their beds of straw,
and clamoring in the life
of an old lamp,
the new fuzzed chicks
tossed their shrill *peep peep*
into the rising joy
of the Easter world.

Watching

Small, behind the sweating horses,
my father turned the hillside
into garden. "Stay back!" he snapped
when I in awful trembling stepped
too near the stepping hooves,
and I stayed back—until, the plowing
done, he sat me on a wide, wet
back and let me ride in harness creak
and glory the long way down the lane
to Baker's farm and the cool barn.
Their labor ended, the horses stamped
and banged their dented buckets
in contented hunger as my father combed
their sweat-caked hair out smooth.
In the yellow light breaking from bulbs
strung along the center beam
Mr. Baker moved in patient ease—
water and oats his single thought.
And in the doorway, watching, I stayed back.

Springhouse

One summer day, flushed red
from climbing apple trees,
I swung the wooden door
heavy with dampness back
against the stone wall
and entered the dark coolness
flowing from the hill.

Over the square pool
so clear it seemed to be
almost not there, I knelt.
I bent and cupped my hands.

Outside, in the light,
familial voices rippled
like water before me.

I drank and drank—
I rose filled beyond thirst.

Housefire

Outside my window, darkness filled
the woods like the afternoon
whir of cicada song.
The light glowed in the trees—
sunset after starfall.

I lay in my bed awake, knowing,
beyond the edge of sleep,
my dream of fire awaited
my surrender. Before its fingers
touched my cheek or clasped my hand,
Father came, lifted, and carried me
to the car where Mother sat,
my brother in her arms.

But he was not fleeing fire.

He climbed the hill behind the house
and drove into the glow.
At the crest he stopped.
Below us a house burned.
Its skin was gone.

Flames lit up its skeleton side
turning men and trucks
to shadows. I looked into the light
and all my dark was fire.

Earthmover

My father's work was driving hi-lift,
carving foundations from the earth.

When Dot and Frank chose to build
a squat, brick house at the lane's end,
he drove a Cat home. At our door,
he stopped, reached down an arm,
and raised me to his side.

High on the sun-cracked seat,
Earthmover, I tugged and pushed
the levers with all my weight.

Through a cloud of diesel blue
the Cat clattered out Leax Lane.
Throned, at the heart of noise,
I loved my father's work.

Dark

The chicken house came down
when Pap started dying.

One summer night Butch pitched
a tent on the level
where it had stood and announced,
"We're sleeping out."

He was eleven. I was six.
I can't remember who got scared first.

But the sharp distinction
between the natural dark
and the mellow, human light
in the house fell
like dew on our wakefulness.

We fled together
and huddled in the light
of Pap's mocking grin.

The dark, however, ruled the day:

Pap died.

Women's Work

It was always dark in grandmother's house
and cool. If I'd come in
on summer days to hide from light,
she'd give me women's work—
a package of Oleo, fresh from the store.
I'd take the bag of stark,
white vegetable fat, place my thumbs
upon the color dot, a splotch of red
like the bloodspot on my breakfast egg,
and knead the soft lipid
until I held a table spread,
yellow, appetizing, fit for the
white of bread.

Outside the house, a cocker bitch,
black and mean, slept, a dreaming guard
at her door. Once when I reached out
to wake her—I woke her—she turned,
fierce canines ripping white,
slashing my wrist to bone.
And I stood speechless, my blood
like springwater flowing, flowing
onto the ground.

Another day, when I was mowing grass,
my brother, on hands and knees
(but obstinate in his will) beside
her peonies, refused to yield the way

to me. I rammed the mower forward
catching his fingers in the whirling
reel; blood sprayed like grass
clippings, incarnadine in air.
That night, caned and chastened, I
begged forgiveness. I held his hands,
bandaged white, in mine. I worked
the bloodspots in the gauze
but failed to knead away the stains
my fingers wore.

II

BURNING

Burning burning burning burning
O Lord Thou pluckest me out
O Lord Thou pluckest
burning

T. S. Eliot, "The Fire Sermon"

1.

Three years
before my mother
followed my father
into Calvin's fold
and set the angry fires
of Pap's Catholic heart
flaming,
water from a priest's finger
insured
I would not burn.

2.

From the top of the steps
my aunt waved to my mother
at the bus stop.

Fifteen months awkward,
I spilled headfirst from the porch
into the bottles
set out for return
and screamed.

Blood burst from my eyes.
Half the world turned red
and half the world went out.

My aunt turned,
wailed to my mother,
and scooped me from the glass.

All the way to the hospital
Pap held me bleeding on his lap.

3.

In the upstairs bedroom
where I sometimes slept,
three terrors
kept me quiet
in my bed.

Across from me
St. Thomas, repenting
his common sense,
fingered the wounds of Christ.

And over my head,
where I never looked,
Christ himself
hung splayed and dying.

From under the bed
the faint reek of a half-rinsed pot.

4.

After a day on the B & O,
Pap settled in his corner chair
and poured an Iron City—
or was it Duke?
I can't remember.

But ah
the taste
of the foam.
That I remember.
Drinking.
Drinking the foam.

5.

Whitewashed catalpa trees
graced the sideyard.
But nightmares
as well as boys
roamed between their trunks.
Pap's turtles, reluctant, cold pets
with dates carved in their shells,
strained against taut,
tethering wires.
Their fowl beaks
snapped sharply
at fat mosquitoes
gorged with blood.

And as the dark closed in,
the sky over Braddock
turned red from the mills
where men stoking the furnaces
of Hell stripped
to the waist
and glistened in their fire-lit sweat.

The doors across the street opened.
Laughter and jazz
washed over us like waves of heat.

Grandma motioned me inside,
but my eye stayed fixed,
intent,
on black flashing thighs.

6.

Twice in four years
the debate swelled.

Pap swore by Stevenson.
My father,
fresh from Germany,
liked Ike.
My mother took his side.

Flung by animosities
deeper than their argument
their words
slashed the air
and set the turtle wires
whining.

When Pap's anger rose
to violence,
we were banished
to the car
and told
to keep the windows up.

Through the panes
and darkening night,
we watched
love wage silent war
with love.

7.

When pap quit the railroad,
retired,
he sold his big house
and moved back down the hill
to the house
he'd one son
and four daughters before
outgrown.

My father,
working after work
with me for company,
had done the renovation.

But even his skill
at carpentry,
his new wood and paint
could not clear
the air.

My every entry
was a shock—
a recognition
of stale Mail Pouch
and ways beyond
my knowing.

8.

The house stood
attic, two rooms up
and two rooms down
in the hillside.

The front porch,
a balcony
built above
the coal cellar,
leaned over the road.

From there
on sticky Pittsburgh
evenings
we watched
the flames of war
consume the south
of Scarlet O'Hara
on the drive-in screen
across the valley.

Carloads of blacks
oblivious to history
roared, radios blaring,
around the corner
heading up the hill.

"God damned jigaboos!"
Pap muttered
and spit
a thick brown stream
into the weeds.

9.

"The yard's
a dangerous place,"
Pap said.

"There was this guy
I knew.

"One day coupling boxcars,
he got careless
and fell.
He fell on his feet,
but the couplers
got him.

"Closed right
around his waist.

"Well, he
stood there
calm as could be
smoking
a cigarette
until they got
the couplers loose.

"Then, by God,
his guts
dumped out
and he dropped
dead on the spot."

10.

The night looked dark to Pap.
He did not go gently.
But I was not there.
I had not been there for years.
I cannot speak.

I'm told death tried him
sorely
and lost.

I'm told he sweltered
in his bed,
turned black
like curling paper
before it bursts into flame.

I'm told before he sensed
the limits of his strength,
the strength of his need,
he scared the family
into prayer.

I'm told he died
burnt out
but smiling.

11.

No one wanted the house
wracked by memories
and decline.

A slumlord
who didn't mind
the leaking
roof or toilet
made the only offer.

Before the deal
was closed,
mysteriously,
as several times
before houses
on the hill
had died,

flames licked
the taste
of fading must
from the walls
and pulled the roof
into their clasp.

12.

If flames refine
and do not burn,
if they consume
the dross
and leave the gold,

then in that ground
beneath the charred
and ruined shell
a single nugget

sleeps

awaiting the landlord
who will pay
the purchase price
and set
what's left
in order.

III

THIRST

1.

No drought threatened
my father's land.

But when the dowser walked a grid
across the plot, the forked branch
gripped lightly in his hands
held steady in the air.

No flowing water would make
our habitation easy;
our lives would be sustained
by guile or skill.

To live by skill
required discipline,
the imposition of limits
before the imposition
of the end.

Habituated to the faucet's flow,
our minds could not acknowledge
the terms of earth.

We chose to live by guile.

2.

The knowledge of Cats,
of diesel engines
and digging deep
straight walls,
lived in my father's hands.

The big bucket clanging,
blue smoke chuffing
from the stack, he cut
fifteen feet into the shale.

He built a chambered cistern
larger than our whims.
But when the water passed
the level of enough,
the weight of excess
cracked the floor.

Brokenness returned
our minds to skill.
We learned to do
with little.

3.

When winter rains
turned to blizzards
and the pump sucked air,
we hauled the lid aside
and shoveled snow
into the hole.

It mounded to the roof,
and we dropped
into the glow of snowy light
and threw the brightness
deeper into dark.

Hour after hour
we sweated warm
to drink depths
below the reach of frost.

4.

The year it snowed on Easter
Father died before
the first purple crocus
affirmed the cyclic
resurrection of the year.

The cistern crack
heaved like a fault,
and our water ran
into the shale.

5.

I climbed into the dry dark.

The square of light
falling on the floor
revealed the flaw,
the wild scrawl
or unbridled ambition.

In half-light, I picked
the thin line open wide
and stuffed the fissure
with waterplug.

My father's shadow
darkening my labor,
I knew the wealth
of water he imagined
could not be held.

I worked to stay the flow
enough to live
from rain to rain.

6.

Nights later an early storm
swept up the valley.

At dawn I rose,
went out,
and hand over hand
lowered the measuring pole
into the dark.

In sunlight I read
the limit of my thirst
and vowed
to make enough
enough.

IV

HERE

As we grow older
The world becomes stranger, the pattern more complicated
Of dead and living.

T. S. Eliot, "East Coker"

Here

Here is the place of order
made by daily labor.
Against bright sky, the house,
limned by spruce and larch,
grown old in weathered caring,
stands white. Beyond its shadow,
the garden lies down in rows
stretched fondly on the earth.
Forsythia and honeysuckle,
lilac, lily, and blueberry
hedge define commitment's
reach. Within its bounds
dwarf apples promise cider
mulling on the winter stove,
and we, faithful, bound
flesh to flesh, learn
in brokenness the changes
love works in fertile soil.

Witness

Broken two summers ago when
a workman, driven against his will,
backed a Cat into its branches,
the dogwood still unfolded white
in April. Its four-petaled leaves,
each touched with the blood
of Christ, shone like lamps.
All spring we followed its brilliance
home and gloried in its light.

Now in October, berry rich and
budded, bearing the deepest red of all
our trees, it stands a silent
wounded sentinel, witness
to the falling gold of larch.

By the Compost Bin

By the compost bin—
   an old spade upright
in the earth!

Fire

We've stacked ten cords of wood
against the falling dark
and sealed the windows tight
to thwart the cold.

Twenty years of steady burning
have taught us how
to keep a bed of coals
intense and deep.

Our care is master of the night.
Let winter come;
our smallest breath
can kindle flame.

Before Christmas

From Remnant Acres
I've culled
deadwood—
fallen hemlock
and poplar.

It weighs so little!

The fire desires
it like air.

Already I've tracked
the carpet thin
between the woodpile
and the stove.

Gift Catalogue

For my wife and daughter
I have bought gifts
I must not name for they wait
unopened beneath the tree.

For my mother I have sent
a light so she can walk
without fear through
the dark of loneliness.

For my brother I have made
a book, the story of a boy's entry
into the truth of his salvation.

For my sister I have reached out
and given the failure of my voice.

For you, my friends, I have sat
before the frightening page
and shaped these words
to celebrate the child
born this night into the suffering
and sorrow of our lives.

But for that child I have ought
to give for all I have
is His. I give Him then
nothing—
the emptiness of my heart
for His local habitation.

The Christmas Ax

a new ax
    to cleave oak
to split it clean
    to open my mind
like heartwood

a new ax
    to fit my hands
to wear callouses
    on my palms
and make them shine

a new ax
    to wield with care
to loose from the tree
    the new man
born in fire

Advent Dinner

A gift it cost us nothing
to share, we brought our turkey
to your table and sat,
as once before in need we sat,
graced by the light
of your home.

Beside my plate, in the midst
of abundance, I found a dish
of pickles, homemade and crisp,
dark with flavor.

I ate them like candy, their
sharp crunch stinging my tongue.
You laughed that I chose
such wafers from the wealth spread
before me. "Pickles!"
you cried. "We've got pickles!"
And you left the table.
Moments later, you returned
laden with jars rich with
summer's plunder for me
to carry home.

Today, two days after New Year's,
I speared the last dark
gherkin from the brine
and tongued again the sharpness
of friendship, the crisp
tang of earth's body.

These words, an earnest against
another advent, I say for you,
a sign of feasts to come.

The Rose

On Remnant Acres the apple trees
are thicker than my trunk.
Gnarled, twisted by neglect
and wind, they rise to light
above the threatening scrub.
Small, yellow apples, spotted
and knobby grow out of reach.
Each fall, I pick them
from the ground, eat what
brief appetite requires
and leave the rest for deer
to root from snow.

But here, in the garden, where
dwarf trees have names—Cortland,
Delicious, and Spy—
I shape a trust in winter
cold with pruning shears, cut
heaven seeking branches and feed them
to the fire. The limber,
earth swooping branches bear
my hope, the rose hidden
deep in the fruit of Eden.

Stilling Death

The butchered chickens flapped,
blood spurting,
through the weeds.

Dauntless in pursuit,
I covered their flights
with a stained bushel basket
and contained their thrashing
by my weight.

I took delight in stilling death.

Tonight, forty years
from that thumping against my thighs,
I split kindling with the hatchet
that cleaved their heads
and clutch, at last, in my grasping hand
the weight of ritual,
the wild exchange,
the blood life

that lives in me.

A Blessing

On a warm
day I
gathered

pruned limbs
(rabbit gnawed
to green-

white wood)
from melting
snow

and blessed
(where they
lay about

the drip
line)
round

pellets
charged with
life.

Morning

Over the crusted
snow, curled leaves
(fallen

from the last
wood
pile)

flame
like a new
fire—

the crackling
applause
to the first

breaking
of the year
into birdsong.

The Process

Between winter
and spring

the first
crocus breaks

into light
into words.

Floodcrest

Through March, rain
beat its steady rhythm
on the taut skin
of our lives.

When, at last,
fear of the river's
crest drove me out
to meet the rise,
I found the surge
contained. The long
dry earth received the
flow and held it fast
in the darkness
of her body.

This morning, the sun
broke from the clouds,
drenched the leafless
woods in light
and loosed this song

urge upon urge upon urge.

Closed Couplet

The year ends in April not December;
I sit alone, and I remember.

Dream

My father was with me.
In my new car, an Escort wagon,
we turned up Brown Avenue
out of Turtle Creek and headed home
to Leax Lane.

The engine, running like a dream,
purred as we sped past Sunday drivers.
Cruising the long straight-a-way
from Bill Free's, where my father worked,
to the White Horse Inn, where I played
pinball with Butch, I asked,
"Do you think we might get
some fishing in this summer?"

"A couple days," my father said.
"We can go up the river."

Then we reached Leax Lane.
All the mailboxes were shiny new.
Aunt Dot's had nothing in it.
Our's bore someone else's name.

I didn't notice until later
that Baker's barn was gone.

Starting up the lane, the car
lost power. I downshifted
and lurched forward, but halfway
up the hill in front of Mrs. Lackatoss's
house the engine died.

"Something wrong?" my father asked.

"The car," I said.
"I can't get up the lane."

Angry I got out. Grasping the front
bumper, as if I grasped the bridle
of a balking horse, I pulled.

"Come on," I cried. "Move."

Then from his seat my father
gently spoke. "I'm sorry,"
he said. "You seem to have
forgotten. I'm dead.
The lane is closed."

Easter Morning

In the cornfield
where winter thin
deer have browsed,

a single tractor
growls slowly
back and forth.

Behind it the
earth, like an
old grave, opens.

Waking

Only that day dawns to which we are awake.

Henry David Thoreau

In the green glow
of sunlight breaking
through the translucent
roof of the Fillmore
Mill, swallows spear
from the rafters,
flash like points
of joy before
my eyes. Caught
in the reckless
abandon of their
flight, I breathe
deep the thick,
sweet air of promise
and wake, filled
with a wild cheeping
into spring.

A Clarity

In spring
peepers
crawl reeds

and shrill
the night
full.

By flash-
light I've
watched

their
throats
balloon

transparent
as their
need.

Spring Shower

This spring shower makes
the sound of spilling grain
each drop a seed
to be ground into flour
and baked into bread.

It is the body of the Lord.

Tilling the Garden

With hands winter soft
and burning,
I horse the tiller
across the garden.

Before me, my father
and his father
performed this task
in the quiet
of harness creak
and hoofplod.

Conceiving joy,
I labor by will
in the presence
of those
who labored
out of need.

The soil, indifferent,
loosens
to receive the seed.

Planting Beets

My knees sink into the earth
as I bend over the row.
My joy is made in risk—
the garden's promise
of nothing sure.

The soil in my hand
is dark. It crumbles
through my fingers and falls
covering the coarse seed
I've laid down the bed.

At dusk, speaking to no one
who will hear, I tongue
the body's hope—
the blood-veined green,
the gritty richness of the leaf.

Filleting the Catch

An extension of my hand,
the supple blade slips
along the dorsal fin
and rides the rib cage
to the tail.
There is no blood
until I cut deep
into the body
behind the flaming gills.
Even then there is little
to redden the clean beauty
of white flesh
lifting from tiny bones.

Seedbed

All day I labored
heaving railroad ties,
setting down a dark
line of division
between garden and field.

Now, at nightfall,
I come, muscle-tense
and tight, to the judgment
of your grace. Lost,
I yield my husband's

need to order. I learn
the joyful wholeness
of earth's body,
my garden
and my field.

V

REMNANT ACRES

The goal of work is not to gain wealth and possessions, but to serve the common good and bring glory to God.

Richard Foster, *Freedom of Simplicity*

Remnant Acres

The apples of the old orchard, plagued
by sucker growth, drop windfalls
to seed an order wilder than their rows.

This is the end
of human design.

At the edge of the wood, the wind-
toppled hemlock rests on still supple
branches for snow to bear it down.

This is the birth
like death.

And in the ruined field the popple
stand shades the dying briars, becomes
a grove of pale green quavering in wind.

This is renewal, the word
spoken in earth.

Clearing Trail

The clearing, cut
by another
to hold a house,
is grown thick
with scrub.

No one will
soon live here.

My labor is
to claim
what the woods
give up,
no more.

With scythe, ax,
and shovel
I write a
crooked line for
you to follow
through berry tangle,
scat, and popple
sprout.

Writing Shack

The old camper, nosed
into a grove of ash 100 yards
from School Farm Road,
has come to rest.

From its vantage I can see
the near lights of town,
the lives of friends burning
through the night.

Or I can turn,
walk into the dark,
and attend the starfire
blazing in the spring.

Here, surrounded by saplings
as comely as young girls,
I say the small peace
broken words can make.

In Such Light

The spring we paid the price
to set this place apart,
we came early and spread
a blanket under the century-
old maple at the wood's edge.
When we lay down together,
sunlight, filtered through a
wavering mesh of green-fringed
branches, fell on your face.
The sharp line along your cheek,
the demarcation between earth and wife,
dissolved in a changing pattern
of shadow. Leaves, curled brown,
pungent with their descent
into humus, found your hair.
Your breath gave life
to summer, and I rose, the maple
swaying over you, alive in such
light as earth can know.

Chosen Work

Before my scythe, weeds, finger-thick
thornapples, and raspberry canes
fall tearing at my arms and legs.
Not born to this work, I learn
rhythm as I go. Though I will know
an ache deep enough to keep me
waking long past the tiredness
of my body's cry for sleep, a dream
drives me. I work to clear
a thicket grown impenetrable
in the scar of failed ambition.
Sparing popple, cherry, and maple,
I work to make what once was here
be here again. Behind me, in the
earth broken by stump-hole and dozer
track, the saplings stand up
in light. Wind turns their leaves
to rain. In their life I live
and know this labor is not vain.

Prayer

Let this slow labor
bring light to earth.

Let the young ash stand
free of thornapple shade.
Let the bloodroot
beneath it blossom.

Let the cords of wood
culled for the quick
destruction of fire
dry in sunlight

And the brush pile
settling into itself
shelter fidgeting birds,
rabbits, and mice.

Let what is done here
in the solitude of need
be done well, be done
for the good of earth.

And the good of one
on whom the earth depends.

Will

Along the fence row, horses crop
the edge of Remnant Acres,
but where neither fence nor stake
marks the boundary of the wood,
the trees have begun their ragged
march into the field. Before
them the order of farmers
and the schemes of agents who plot
the earth for sale will fall.
By right of ownership I give
consent to trees, by choice
check the willfulness that cries,
"What is, is mine to order." But
too soon I will lie down among
roots and yield up my refusal
to hold back. After me another
chooses. What limits he may will
I cannot know. To his willing
hands I will my husbandry.

What Earth Gives

From winter brightness I descended
into the deep, gully shadow
where the stream, turning, carves
the hill away. Across my path
I found a hemlock, its roots
torn free by swollen waters,
the sudden runoff of an autumn
storm. Beneath it two green
ashes lay broken by its fall.
Over these, waiting the flood
of spring, a great cherry leaned.
By water's grace I need fell
no trees. Yet I will earn
my warmth, for what earth gives
must be claimed in sweat—
the hard bearing of the weight
uphill to hammer and wedge,
the long haul home.

Winter Spring

In the ravine bottom,
where the hemlocks
shade the stream, the still
water is frozen. But
halfway up the bank,
the tiny pool I made
last spring, when I walked
the flow to its beginning,
is open. A constant
source of falling water,
a still small voice
beneath the trees, it pours
burbling from the hill's
side, *I am I am.*

Please

Give me a bowl
of that soup
you've made with
cabbage, potatoes,
and many carrots.

I'm just back from
Remnant Acres, where
I've been splitting
twisted maple butt.
It ate my wedges
and wore me down.

Give me that good
nourishment your hands
provide. Sit with me
while I ask a blessing
on our day. All
we need is here.

Atonement

Before the snap of spring
brought the sap surging
to the tight leafbuds
of the age-barren apples,
I filled the wood
with chainsaw drone
and snarled the deer-
trail path with fallen trees.

The quick violence done,
I kept the slow labor
of cutting firewood free
to bring me back
and turned to other
work, to students
wanting words to make
a clarity come true.

In jay squall I returned
with handsaw, ax, and shears
to limb and stack
the tangle. Confusion
yielded to my hands—
brush fell like useless words
from trying compositions
a compost for the wood.

As it fell it shaped two
works: the woodpile stayed
against the freezing night,
the wood itself restored.
By grace these two are one.
By grace they shape a
clarity: the workman
broken and made whole.

Who Could Ask For More?

When lightning split a two-cord limb
from the trunk and left the maple
scarred, misshapen and dangerous,
I brought it down. Its fall
swept two hemlocks, a green ash
and an apple gone wild before it.
All summer I worked to clear
the tangle of tops, cutting and stacking,
in sweat thinking of winter cold.
Now on an autumn afternoon,
as you recline against the stump
in the center of the opening
I have made, I rest my head
on your thigh. The sun, stronger than
the wind driving clouds across the sky,
warms my body that is not
what it was when first I lay
beside you on a winter night,
but touch has taught us touch,
and all that flesh can give
is ours. We lie in this clearing
in time, content, blessed
by light falling like leaves.

Country Labors
was set in Goudy Old Style
by the Composition Department
of Zondervan Publishing House,
Nancy Wilson, compositor.
Text design by Bob Hudson.
Cover design by the Aslan Group, Ltd.
Printing by Malloy Lithographing
of Ann Arbor, Michigan.